BEFORE *the* STORM

PRE-STORM STRATEGIES

DR. MICHAEL FREEMAN

FREEMAN PUBLISHING
MARYLAND

Freeman Publishing
2261 Oxon Run Drive
Temple Hills, MD 20748
freemanpublishing@sofcc.org

Printed in the United States of America

Scripture quotations identified NLT are from the Holy Bible, New Living Translation © 1996, 2004, 2007, 2013 by Tyndale House Foundation. Used by permission of Tyndale House Publishers Inc., Carol Stream, Illinois 60188. All rights reserved.

Scripture quotations identified NKJV are from the New King James Version®. Copyright © 1982 by Thomas Nelson. Used by permission. All rights reserved.

Author photography by Clark Bailey Photography
Book cover design by Chantee The Designer LLC

Library of Congress Cataloging-in-Publication data
ISBN 978-1-944406-02-8

This book is dedicated to my mother, the late Carrie B. Freeman. She was my first example of faith. She taught me how to live by faith.

She always saw more in me than I saw in myself. I am committed to continuing her legacy of being a Gold Digger. I promise to always dig for the best in everyone I come in contact with.

Lastly to my wife, DeeDee, in the words of a profound songwriter that I know (smile), "I wouldn't want to do life without you!" I could write an entire second book on you being my Proverbs 31 woman. DeeDee, you showed an amazing level of unwavered strength and faith during my storm, and you haven't looked back. I am excited about what God has in store for you and I! It's nothing short of amazing.

I love you DeeDee!

CONTENTS

Acknowledgements
Introduction

1. Prepare with Prayer

2. Declare Victory

3. Develop a spirit of Faith

4. Win With The Word

5. Re-adjust Your Thought Life

6. Perfect the Love Walk

7. Fail Not to Forgive

Storm Preparation Checklist
About the Author

ACKNOWLEDGEMENTS

To my children, Brittney, Joshua, and Brelyn, thank you for your unquestionable faith in allowing me to lead you as a father. I promise each of you that your obedience will not go unnoticed or rewarded. I couldn't have asked for a better home team!

To Tressa Smallwood, of Power Play Books, thank you for making it happen.

To Natasha Brown, thank you for your consistent diligence to ensure that I get this important word out to the world. The unmeasurable hours you have given to the project is forever appreciated.

To Linda Tyler, thank you for assisting making this project one that I can be proud of. Your contribution is greatly appreciated.

To Chanteé Jackson, thank you for lending your time and talent in the design and creation of the book cover. Your eye for creativity is absolutely amazing. You making your pastor look really handsome (lol)!

To my father, Bishop Robert O. Freeman, the greatest example of humility that I know. From birth until now, and even until eternity, I will always be grateful for you.

To my Pastor, Apostle Dr. Frederick K.C. Price, thank you for teaching me, through word and example, how to walk by faith. I credit a vast majority of the success of my life and ministry to your unwavering stand to exemplify faith.

To all of the physicians at the Washington Hospital Center and Laurel Regional Hospital, thank you for your superb attention to detail to ensure I was taken care of and comfortably rehabilitated.

To Richard and Sophia Smith, thank you for having a heart to take care of my wife during my stay in the hospital. It warmed my heart to know that while I was unable to make sure she was good, she never lacked because of dependable people like you.

To my niece, NiKia Wooten, thank you for making sure I received the proper treatment in the best facility. More importantly, thank you for being sensitive to the Holy Spirit.

To Keshia Williams, thank you for looking out for your pastor. Because of your heart in not wanting me to wait, you literally saved my life!

BEFORE THE STORM

Everything was going perfectly well. There was no forecast to warn you. You could not have predicted it. Then suddenly, without invitation or reservation, it was there; the unexpected storm. In life there will be storms, but if you are prepared *before the storm*, the strong winds and roaring thunder will not cause you to become fearful and anxious.

Think about it for a moment. Have you ever experienced a storm in your life that arose out of nowhere? Well, if you have or find yourself facing a storm right now, pay close attention, because your pre-storm strategy boot camp is about to begin. Let me lay the foundation with the case of the twelve disciples. There they were with Jesus, in the middle of the lake, when a violent storm arose. Before this storm, Jesus had been teaching a group of people by the sea. The Bible does not mention clouds in the sky or winds stirring up during that entire day. It tells us that when evening came, Jesus told His disciples that it was time to cross the sea to the other side. This leads us to conclude that the weather was seemingly perfect for sailing, and there was no sign of a storm in the near future. However, soon after they set sail they were met with a storm. Before the storm, Jesus decided to go to sleep in the bottom of the boat and was still asleep when the disciples found themselves in trouble.

"On the same day, when evening had come, He said to them, "Let us cross over to the other side." Now when they had left the multitude, they took Him along in the boat as He was. And other little boats were also with Him. And a great windstorm arose, and the waves beat into the boat, so that it was already filling. But He was in the stern, asleep on a pillow. And they awoke Him and said to Him, "Teacher, do You not care that we are perishing?" Then He arose and rebuked the wind, and said to the sea, "Peace,

be still!" And the wind ceased and there was a great calm.

But He said to them, "Why are you so fearful? How is it

that you have no faith? And they feared exceedingly, and

said to one another, "Who can this be, that even the wind

and the sea obey Him!"

Mark 4:35-41

Like the disciples, people often panic when unforeseen storms arise. They begin to worry, feeling like the situation is impossible to overcome. The disciples were concerned that Jesus, the One Who could solve their problem, was asleep during the storm, and they even questioned whether He cared about what they were going through. This is relative to us, even today. As Christians, we may go through storms in life and feel alone because it appears as if Jesus is "sleeping." We see in the passage above that this could not be further from the truth. In the face of tragedy, adversity, and crisis, Jesus is right there with us. He promised that He would be with us in trouble. Psalm 46 says that He is a present help in the time of trouble. That means that He is not just there, He is an active participant. If you will allow Him, He is there to calm your storm just like He did for the disciples that night in the boat, but you must trust Him.

My objective is to help you "sleep" like Jesus did. The last thing many people think to do during a crisis is rest. However, when you know that the King of kings and the Lord of lords is with you that is exactly what you should do; give your cares to Jesus and rest. You have the ability to take on the mind of Christ and the faith of Christ, even in your most difficult circumstances. What you are about to learn are strategies that will allow you to sleep during your storm. You will be calm, without a worry or fear just like Jesus, and you will conquer any adverse situation that you may encounter.

You may remember one storm in particular that had devastating effects on countless lives. Hurricane Katrina tormented the Gulf Coast on August 25, 2005. When the storm made landfall, it had a Category 3 rating on the Saffir-Simpson Hurricane Scale; it brought sustained winds of 100 –140 miles per hour and stretched 400 miles across. The storm itself did a great deal of damage, but its aftermath was catastrophic. Levee breaches led to massive flooding, and many people were angry that the federal government seemed slow to meet the needs of the people affected by the storm. Hundreds of thousands of people in Louisiana, Mississippi and Alabama were displaced from their homes. Unlike the storm that the disciples faced, Hurricane Katrina was forecasted. The storm brewed for a week and 24 hours before Hurricane Katrina attacked the Gulf Coast, New Orleans Mayor Ray Nagin declared that the inhabitants of the city must evacuate. There was little time to prepare and as a result, the poor, the elderly, the sick and those without transportation found themselves stuck in the middle of a catastrophe.

Before the deadly storm, meteorologists forewarned residents of the danger. I imagine that essentially everyone who lived on the Gulf Coast was aware that the storm was on its way. In fact, weather experts had tracked the growing tropical storm for over a week while it was still in the Bahamas, making its way to the states. By August 28, just a day before the storm, people were still in the region. The National Weather Service predicted that after the storm hit, "most of the [Gulf Coast] area would be uninhabitable for weeks….perhaps longer."

Hurricane Katrina and its aftermath were far worse than what the people envisioned. The city was declared a disaster zone. I remember the sickening images of men and women trapped in a city under water. Eight percent of New Orleans was underwater at some point. An angry city, region and nation began to blast the Bush Administration for its slow response. Damages soared into the billions and worst of all, people lost hope in their chances and ability to ever rebuild after that storm. No one could have stopped Mother Nature or altered the course of the storm; but it was evident that the region had not properly prepared for Hurricane Katrina. America had in fact failed New Orleans because it failed to prepare before the storm.

Both storms mentioned above—the storm that Jesus encountered, and the lessons learned from Hurricane Katrina, should not be reduced to mere weather accounts or natural disasters. Instead, they teach us an important spiritual lesson which is to expect the storm and prepare in advance. Notice that the storm that Jesus was in, ended successfully. The disciples and Jesus were able to continue on their path, almost uninterrupted by that storm. On the contrary, in the Hurricane Katrina disaster, the leaders essentially lacked preparation which ended with massive deaths, controversy and ruins.

After the storm hits, it is too late to prepare for the storm. The time for preparation has passed. However, this is how most believers respond to the adverse situations in their lives. After they have been attacked, that is when they start to gather scriptures on how to endure the storm or increase their prayer life. Most of the time, it is simply too late. If you do not have what you need before you "go through," you will never make it through.

During Hurricane Katrina, New Orleans' primary focus was on the decaying foundation opposed to the dilapidated levees which caused most of the flooding. Many believers get in trouble, because they were not listening or paying attention. Instead of preparing ahead of time, and fixing what is broken, many of us ignore the cracks and when a storm comes it causes catastrophic damage that in most instances could have been diverted.

Anything that is not in order, is out of order and God is not obligated to participate. Unfortunately, a lot of us have been doing things that have been out of the order of God and are wondering why His spiritual principals are not having an impact.

If we want God's best, it is important that we align ourselves with the kingdom of God in order to guarantee that everything the bible says about us and what God has planned for us comes to pass.

If you live in America, you might recall that when a storm is developing in your region, your local news station will have an interruption from the Emergency Broadcasting System. That warning always disturbs whatever television show you are watching and flashes across your screen to inform you of what is to come. There is a loud beeping sound and often the broadcast cuts to your local meteorologist who begins to analyze the speed, rate, estimated arrival of the storm and how long it will last.

In life however, most storms are not preceded by loud interruptions. No one can foresee how many people will be affected, and no one can predict how long the storm will last. As we learned from Hurricane Katrina, the aftermath of the storm is more crucial than the actual storm itself. People spend years, decades and the remainder of their lives rebuilding what was lost—when they have failed to prepare properly. As I thought about the concept and formation of storms, I realized that without the alerts or an expert who can predict these life-threatening emergencies, there are very few warning signals. However, as believers, we have the advantage; God has provided us with the Word that tells us that we should always be prepared.

According to John 16:33, we all have an evil day associated with our names: but the good news is......the evil day does not have to overtake you. My own evil day has mirrored this truth. A few years ago, my family and I were preparing to go on a beautiful vacation, when an unexpected storm hit all of our lives. A routine morning in my home turned into three hard months of life-threatening surgeries, followed by an unexpected—but miraculously speedy—rehabilitation process. There were no warning signs or abrupt interruptions on my television to inform me that this storm was coming my way. Although I did not intend to go through this storm, unlike the Hurricane Katrina situation, I did prepare ahead of time. My 30 plus years of living by my faith enabled me to withstand the storm during the worst time of my life.

Consider this book Before the Storm your warning; this is your emergency alert. The Bible talks specifically about "an evil day" for us all. Ephesians 6:13 instructs us to, "Therefore take up the whole armor of God, that you may be able to withstand in the evil day, and having done all, to stand." You must be prepared if you want to be standing in the end, and when your foundation is strong enough to withstand the hurricanes and blizzards of life, you will be prepared for anything. No matter what storm comes your way, you will have the full armor of God and the spiritual weapons of warfare serving as the pillars that will make sure you do not break. Remember this, when we have failed to prepare prior to a storm, the pressure can blow us around to and fro, like a loose leaf detached from its tree or unstable levees overwhelmed by water. I overcame my storm and outlived the "evil day" that threatened my life and if it happened for me, it can happen for you. The difference from my "evil day" and yours comes down to being equipped. This one simple factor determines if you win, lose or learn from your storm. You don't have to lose, if you learn.

There are a number of spiritual exercises that I would recommend for you to integrate into your daily life. In fact, they will enable you to emerge victorious, no matter the pressure, obstacles or downpour of negativity that attempt to enter into your life. These exercises are God's way of building our spiritual muscles and making us strong Christians ready for warfare in the spiritual and natural worlds.

The pages that follow are your boot camp preparation guide, so that you will be more than ready to conquer any storm you are facing or will be facing. Let this book serve as your warning and prep kit. A storm is coming, and here is how you get into formation. In these pages, I'm presenting to you my personal practices and principals which allowed me to win the faith fight over time, and again throughout storms in my life. These methods saved my life, allowed my wife to stand firm on the Word, and provided my children with "perfect peace" throughout the process. These strategies will provide you with confidence and spiritual strength. You will never again doubt whether or not you will win the war, or make it through the storm, because you will be prepared *Before the Storm*.

1

PREPARE WITH PRAYER

"Now in the morning, having risen a long while before daylight, He went out and departed to a solitary place; and there He prayed." Mark 1:35

Jesus started everything in His life with prayer and since He is our chief example setter, we should do the same. Jesus provides many examples regarding the time of day to pray, how He prayed and how He taught His disciples to pray. These examples serve as a playbook of how to arise victorious in any storm. If we do things the way that He did them, we will have victory in every area of our lives. Jesus' victory came from having a time of communion. "Communion" is a compound word made up of the words, "community" plus "union" or "common" and "union." Jesus had constant communion with His Father, and so should we.

I Thessalonians 5:17 directs us to pray without ceasing. This means that we should be praying when we rise in the morning, while we are brushing our teeth, in the shower, before we make a phone call or speak in public, before responding to other's requests, when we get a new idea and when we need a new idea. Throughout the day, all day, we should pray without ceasing.

> **Throughout the day, all day, we should pray without ceasing.**

I am not sure about you, but it would be impossible for me to bow my head and close my eyes if I need to talk with God while I am driving in bumper-to-bumper traffic. There are times during the day when you should set aside alone time with God—time when you can truly speak and listen to your Father. In addition, there are other times, when you should just be speaking with Him and communing with Him. During those times, don't worry about how to pray or if you are praying correctly. God does not care about form or fashion. He just wants us to pray continually.

The Bible tells us of how Jesus went to the mountains to pray. For us, this translates to spending alone time with God, so that we can hear His voice. Jesus was very honest with God. He asked for what He wanted, and He also surrendered to God's will. Take a look at the example we get from Jesus in Matthew 26:39:

"He went a little farther and fell on His face, and prayed, saying, "O My Father, if it is possible, let this cup pass from Me; nevertheless, not as I will, but as You will."

It is important to petition God, just as Jesus did, but at the root of everything you pray, you must surrender to God's will. One certain way to find peace is through prayer and submission to God's will.

When the disciples said, "Master, teach us how to pray,"

Jesus answered them, not with a prayer, but an outline for prayer. This outline is commonly referred to as "The Lord's Prayer." I find that this was a simplified outline for prayer, which is important, but for a model, we should actually refer to John 17. This passage is a model for prayer before a storm. Jesus prayed for Himself, His disciples and the world before His storm. Jesus' prayer in John 17 has three parts. In verses 1-5, He prayed for Himself, gives honor to God, and reminds God of His own purpose and promise:

"Jesus spoke these words, lifted up His eyes to heaven, and said: "Father, the hour has come. Glorify Your Son, that Your Son also may glorify You, as You have given Him authority over all flesh, that He should give eternal life to as many as You have given Him. And this is eternal life, that they may know You, the only true God, and Jesus Christ whom You have sent. I have glorified You on the earth. I have finished the work which You have given Me to do. And now, O Father, glorify Me together with Yourself, with the glory which I had with You before the world was."

In the second part of John 17, in verses 9-19, Jesus prayed for His disciples. He prayed for their strength and that they may have strength to withstand the forces of "the evil one." Here is what He prayed before the storm:

"I pray for them. I do not pray for the world but for those whom You have given Me, for they are Yours. And all Mine are Yours, and Yours are Mine, and I am glorified in them. Now I am no longer in the world, but these are in the world, and I come to You. Holy Father, keep through Your name those whom You have given Me, that they may be one as We are. While I was with them in the world, I kept them in Your name. Those whom You gave Me I have kept; and none of them is lost except the son of perdition, that the Scripture might be fulfilled. But now I come to You, and these things I speak in the world, that they may have My joy fulfilled in themselves. I have given them Your word; and the world has hated them because they are not of the world, just as I am not of the world. I do not pray that You should take them out of the world, but that You

should keep them from the evil one. They are not of the world, just as I am not of the world. Sanctify them by Your truth. Your Word is truth. As You sent Me into the world, I also have sent them into the world. And for their sakes I sanctify Myself, that they also may be sanctified by the truth."

We can learn a lot from this part of the prayer. Jesus prayed truth for the disciples and prayed that God would sanctify them by that truth. A major takeaway is to always pray for God's complete guidance, wisdom and sanctification so that we continue to walk in His truth.

In the final section of this prayer in John 17, in verses 20-26, Jesus prayed for all believers. He prayed for you and I before the crucifixion, in that we might also be blessed and strengthened, and inherit His blessings, simply because we believe in Him:

"I do not pray for these alone, but also for those who will believe in Me through their word; that they all may be one, as You, Father, are in Me, and I in You; that they also

may be one in Us, that the world may believe that You sent Me. And the glory which You gave Me I have given them, that they may be one just as We are one: I in them, and You in Me; that they may be made perfect in one, and that the world may know that You have sent Me, and have loved them as You have loved Me. Father, I desire that they also whom You gave Me may be with Me where I am, that they may behold My glory which You have given Me; for You loved Me before the foundation of the world. O righteous Father! The world has not known You, but I have known You; and these have known that You sent Me. And I have declared to them Your name, and will declare it, that the love with which You loved Me may be in them, and I in them."

Jesus prayed that we would be one in Him and since God always answered His prayers, we know that this powerful prayer covered us. Get excited! You are covered! If you believe that you are one with Christ— the Father, the Son and the Holy Spirit, that means that through Jesus, you are already victorious in anything and everything that you may encounter and you have already defeated the enemy. It is important to understand and truly believe this before the storm.

Jesus was in constant communion with His Father and we as believers must do the same. Before His trial, He could talk freely with Him and pray for a covering for His disciples and all believers. This is the before the storm lesson concerning prayer. Establish consistent communication with God.

Many times satan, the accuser, has an advantage over believers. For instance, if you do not have a prayer life before a storm, he will try to condemn you for your lack of prayer life, while you are in that storm. You will begin to second-guess yourself with thoughts like,"Why am I trying to pray… Before I went through a storm, I never wanted to talk to God… God is not listening now. It is too late. My prayers are pointless." If you are not strong in Christ you will feel defeated, and will not want to talk to God; especially during your crisis. This is why it is important to look at Jesus' example of prayer. Look at these five strategies that Jesus implemented throughout His life.

1. He prayed without ceasing.

2. He spent time alone with God.

3. He did not make a major move in His ministry without God.

4. He did not try to heal anyone without the covering of His Father.

5. He had that constant communion with God.

Do you see where I am going with this information? It is important to constantly communicate with your heavenly Father through the Lord Jesus Christ long before anything tragic happens.

I have felt guilty in the past when my prayer life was not where it needed to be. In those times, when a crisis would come up, I would run straight to God. This attitude of not praying consistently before the crisis is the equivalent of needing something from someone who you refuse to talk to. Go to God, commune with Him, and talk to Him. He loves you and He has everything that you need!

CHOOSING THE RIGHT PRAYER

Have you ever tried to open a locked door with the wrong set of keys or the wrong code? It is not enough just to have the keys; you have to have the right keys in order to gain access to what you want.

There are several prayers that will help prepare you for the storm. It is imperative you understand them all so that you can begin exercising your authority in Christ. As you know, we have been instructed to pray without ceasing. Contrary to how some Christians pray, when you communicate with God through prayer, you do not always have to ask Him for something. The various types of prayers include faith, agreement, intercession, thanksgiving, consecration, and petition. These individual prayers each serve a different purpose. The type

> **When you communicate with God through prayer, you do not always have to ask Him for something.**

of prayer that I have relied on heavily in my life is praying in the spirit, commonly referred to as praying in tongues. Many Christians will debate whether or not praying in the spirit or tongues is necessary, whether or not it is real and if it serves a purpose. The Bible teaches us, through various passages that praying in the spirit/tongues are absolutely real and it serves a specific purpose. That powerful purpose is to communicate in a language that only God and your spirit understand. When we pray in the spirit, we do not have an influence over what we are praying. Our own minds cannot filter our prayers and others (including satan) cannot understand them. Our spirit man, which knows what we need, uses that special language to communicate directly to God on our behalf. Romans 8:26 explains,

"Likewise the Spirit also helps in our weaknesses. For we do not know what we should pray for as we ought, but the Spirit Himself makes intercession for us with groanings which cannot be uttered."

Additionally, we find an explanation for the purpose of speaking in tongues in 1Corinthians 14:2. The Apostle Paul said,

"For he who speaks in a tongue does not speak to men but to God, for no one understands him; however, in the spirit he speaks mysteries."

In the book of Corinthians, the Apostle Paul took a comprehensive approach to conveying the importance of praying with other tongues for various reasons. In 1 Corinthians 14, Paul compared the gifts of prophecy and speaking in tongues, and encouraged other believers to pray more for the gift of prophecy, so that it could be used to uplift one another and the church. In the book of Acts, there are a variety of examples of people who received the Baptism of the Holy Spirit and subsequently the gift of speaking in tongues. In Acts 2, on the day of the Pentecost, *"they were all filled with the Holy Spirit and began to speak with other tongues, as the Spirit gave them utterance."* Then we find in Acts 19, Paul ministered to 12 disciples in Ephesus and asked them if they had received the Holy Spirit since they believed.

Their response was, *"We have not so much as heard whether there is a Holy Spirit."* (Acts 19:1-2). Paul told them about Jesus and the Bible tells us that, *"When they heard this, they were baptized in the name of the Lord Jesus. And when Paul had laid hands on them, the Holy Spirit came upon them, and they spoke with tongues and prophesied"* (Acts 19:1:5).

As you can see from all the scripture references, praying in tongues is essential to an effective prayer life. I also believe that praying in tongues is one of the most important experiences that a believer can have and the most effective type of prayer. Jude 1:20 confirms my belief, *"But you, beloved, building yourselves up on your most holy faith, praying in the Holy Spirit, keep yourselves in the love of God, looking for the mercy of our Lord Jesus Christ unto eternal life."* I spend an incredible amount of time praying in the spirit. I use my heavenly language that has been given to me by God through faith. When we pray in tongues, our spirit prays and we have no understanding of our own because there is a disconnect from our intellect; we are not speaking to man we are speaking to God. It takes faith to speak in other tongues; and although it is something we do not understand, we are still able to participate.

Establishing a prayer life gives us confidence in knowing that if any storm comes our way, we can go boldly before the throne of God and He will help us. God is our refuge and strength, a very present help in trouble (Psalm 46:1).

When you establish this prayer life, you will sometimes be asked to pray for people in situations. Always volunteer to pray for others. Do not say you will pray later. Pray immediately. This is called intercessory prayer. Most people have more confidence in other people's prayer lives than their own, so we must pray for others. One of the most common forms of prayer is petition—or, when we are asking for something of God. You have been told throughout your life to "just pray," or perhaps you are the one who tells others to do so. This is not just empty "spiritual" advice that church people give. According to the Word of God, this specific strategy trumps everything. *"Now this is the confidence that we have in Him, that if we ask anything according to His will, He hears us; and if we know that He hears us, whatever we ask, we know that we have the petitions that we have asked of Him."* (1: John 5:14-15). That scripture is so powerful and in

John 14, Jesus gives us comfort and assurance that we should pray: verse 1: "Let not your heart be troubled; you believe in God, believe also in me." Then in verse 14 Jesus told us that, "If you ask anything in My name, I will do it." Why would you not make prayer your priority? We must prepare for our storms through prayer.

Take special note of how Jesus approached the tomb of Lazarus in John 11:40-44. He did not use empty words or colloquialisms, nor did He pray an emotionally desperate prayer. He prayed efficiently to His Father, "Father, I thank You that You have heard Me. And I know that You always hear Me, but because of the people who are standing by I said this, that they may believe that You sent Me." The

> **The problem with most believers is that they do not have the same confidence in prayer that Jesus did.**

problem with most believers is that they do not have the same confidence in prayer that Jesus did. They do not know for sure, they are just hoping. They say things like 'if it be your Holy will…' The Bible says if we know His will, we ask according to His will and He hears us… so, let us begin to practice that type of prayer life now. The prayer of faith is vitally important in the life of a believer. This means that you believe God's Word as it is written in the Bible. You pray His Word in faith, believing that you have received it, and you fully expect Him to honor His Word.

"Have faith in God," Jesus answered. "Truly I tell you, if anyone says to this mountain, 'Go, throw yourself into the sea, and does not doubt in their heart but believes that what they say will happen, it will be done for them. Therefore I tell you, whatever you ask for in prayer, believe that you have received it, and it will be yours. And when you stand praying, if you hold anything against anyone, forgive them, so that your Father in heaven may forgive you your sins."

Mark 11:22-25

Whenever you pray (according to God's will) and you believe that you have received what you are asking for, then you will have it.

When praying, most people do not demonstrate the prayer of faith. They could have just prayed and got up. Instead they pray and say 'I sure hope I get it,' or they believe that God heard their prayer after He answers their prayer, if they ever believed at all. Well this prayer in Mark 11 says "when you pray," (I repeat) when you pray, meaning at that very moment, while you are praying, believe that you have received those things (believe that you have received them right then and there) and you shall have them! When you are finished, get up, and thank Him in advance for everything that you prayed. You may not physically have it in your hand but believe that it is already in your life. That is why it is a prayer of faith, you believe before you have it.

In Daniel 10:10, Daniel prayed and an angel appeared three weeks later, telling him that the angels actually heard the prayer the very day that he prayed it, but there was a warfare going on in the spiritual realm. As a result, Daniel did not see the manifestation of his prayer for three weeks. Daniel 10:10-14 reads:

> *"A hand touched me and set me trembling on my hands and knees. He said, "Daniel, you who are highly esteemed, consider carefully the words I am about to speak to you, and stand up, for I have now been sent to you." And when he said this to me, I stood up trembling. Then he continued, "Do not be afraid, Daniel. Since the first day that you set your mind to gain understanding and to humble yourself before your God, your words were heard, and I have come in response to them. But the prince of the Persian kingdom resisted me twenty-one days. Then Michael, one of the chief princes, came to help me, because I was detained there with the king of Persia. Now I have come to explain to you what will happen to your people in the future, for the vision concerns a time yet to come."*

We are not moved by what we see; we are moved by what we believe.

2

DECLARE VICTORY

In Luke 8:22, prior to the storm, Jesus went to pray. After He finished praying, He declared to the disciples, *"Let us go over to the other side."* Taking our cue from Jesus, an important pre-storm strategy is to pray and then declare what we want to see, using scriptural references. An example of this would be to declare that: "This will be a great day. I'll be blessed going in and blessed going out. Angels are with me, to keep me in all of my ways. No weapons formed against me shall prosper."

I also use declarations in my salutations. If someone asks me, "How are you doing?" Instead of saying "fine." or "good," I use this as a time to declare, "If I was doing any better, there would have to be two of me!" Always speak positive and that is what you will have. Many people nullify their prayers with their declarations and words so you must be mindful about what is coming out of your mouth after you pray. It is also important to understand that our authority is released by our words. For example, if God would ever call a dog a cat, it would be a cat instantly. Whatever God spoke, that is what it was, and we must speak with that same authority with everything that we say. You cannot open your mouth and say, "I am on a fixed income", because when you do, you just fixed it. The plan that God had for man was that we would have what we say. So let us watch what we say. The late comedian and actor Flip Wilson would say, "What you see is what you get." But with a believer, what you say is what you get." So be mindful of what you declare.

This is a declaration that I created while I was in the midst of a storm. To this day, the declaration that, "We Win," is in my kitchen for my family and I to see every day. Begin now by writing declarations and posting them in places where you will see them each day.

WE WIN!!!

DEUTERONOMY 20:4

FOR THE LORD YOUR GOD IS HE
THAT GOETH WITH YOU, TO FIGHT
FOR YOU AGAINST YOUR ENEMIES,
TO SAVE YOU.

3

DEVELOP A SPIRIT
OF FAITH

"It is written: "I believed, therefore I have spoken – (This is a

declaration)". Since we have that same spirit of faith, we also

believe and therefore speak, because we know that the One

who raised the Lord Jesus from the dead will also raise us with

Jesus and present us with You to Himself."

2 Corinthians 4:13

The magnitude of your success in life is directly connected

to the development of your faith. At the time that you received

Jesus Christ as Lord, you received all the faith that you will ever need to do whatever you have to do in life. No matter what phase of life you are in or what you have done, God created you for a purpose. Before the foundation of the world, He predestined you to carry out a specific assignment. This may come as a surprise to you, but you are not just a product of your parents' passion; you are the product of the purpose of God. Since you have been created with all the faith that you need, all you have to do is develop that faith.

Faith is not hoping, wishing or wondering. It is complete and total trust that God — will not do it— but has already done it. First, let us look at the difference between hope and faith. Dr. Frederick K.C. Price, says that hope is having the right attitude while the ship is sinking. Faith, on the other hand, is knowing that what you have prayed for is already done. Many people live their lives hoping that God will

> **Faith is not hoping, wishing or wondering. It is complete and total trust that God — will not do it— but has already done it.**

make a way, or hoping that God will deliver them from debt or illness, not realizing that they have already failed, and they are actually sinking. Hope is future tense. Faith is now. Hebrews 11:1 says, *"Now faith."* God does not heal us or save us or make us triumphant in a storm because we have great hope. He does this because we have great faith. "I hope God will make a way," is different from knowing and believing that, "God has made a way, and it is already done." I want you to stop hoping and wishing to God like He is some sort of genie in a bottle, and instead put your total faith, confidence and trust in His ability to move on your behalf. Know it to be true, it is already done. Ephesians 1:3 says that God has already given us everything that pertains to His kingdom, *"Blessed be the God and Father of our Lord Jesus Christ, who has blessed us with every spiritual blessing in the heavenly places in Christ..."* Notice that "has" is past tense—it is already done. Both 2 Peter 1:3 and 2 Corinthians 1:20 assure us of this. *"For all the promises of God in Him are Yes, and in Him Amen, to the glory of God through us."* "Yes" and "Amen," that lets us know that it is already done. In other words, your victory over every storm has already been established. You must have faith and believe—versus wavering, hoping and wishing that God may deliver you. The truth is that He has already done it. Now, you simply must walk in a spirit of faith. Let me remind you that when you were born again, you were born with all of the faith that you will need in every situation that you will encounter and that also includes storms (Romans 12:3).

TRUST AND FAITH

Trust and faith in God are so similar, that they are almost synonymous. If you look up the word faith, some Bible dictionaries and concordances will direct you to look at trust, and if you look at trust, they will tell you to look at faith. These two terms are similar, but there is a distinct difference. Trust in God is built through placing your faith in Him. Putting faith in God builds your trust for God. Trust is established over a period of time through faith episodes. By practicing small, daily faith episodes you will eventually find that you are walking by faith, with complete trust in God. Eventually, you will boldly attest. "I have walked by faith long enough and now I am totally in trust mode". One person who trusted God completely as a result of numerous faith episodes was David, the Shepherd Boy.

DEFEATING GOLIATH

In the book of 1 Samuel in the Old Testament, we see David, a shepherd boy, who was responsible for tending to his father's sheep. After David was anointed by Saul (to eventually become king), the Bible tells us that God was with him; and David knew it as well. He never wavered with God or showed an ounce of fear. According to the text, David built his trust in God through repeated faith episodes. Although David was just a youth, he had tended to his father's sheep for many years, and had to regularly protect the herd against lions and bears. These faith episodes led to David's complete trust in God. In one incident, He declared, "The LORD, who delivered me from the paw of the lion and from the paw of the bear, He will deliver me from the hand of this Philistine." (1 Samuel 17:37). Does that sound like David hoped God would deliver him? No, David said with confidence that it is already done! David was the only person among the Israelites who demonstrated enough faith and courage to battle Goliath. He boldly stated, "The battle is the Lord's, and He will give you into our hands." David constantly put his faith in God, and not only did this allow him to develop trust in God, he also had a great deal of trust in his skills. Instead of fighting with the armor that Saul had clothed him with, David used his shepherd's bag, a pouch, a sling, and five pebbles—items that were already in his possession. David knew that the weapon he needed most, the true armor that would defeat Goliath, was on the inside of him; it was the Spirit of God. David also knew how to activate this supernatural power through a spirit of faith. When you are preparing for a storm, it is important to take heed of a few lessons that David's storm teaches us.

1. Once you decide to trust in God, your strength for the fight will come from within.

2. The battle is not yours, it is God's. As long as you are fighting your battle in faith, God will enable you to be triumphant.

Trusting in God means that you have anchored your life in

God. For example, when a ship is anchored, it may drift a little when harsh winds or waves come, but it will never be separated from that anchor. It is set and sturdy. Some have bigger boats than they have anchors, meaning that they have built their lives bigger than the trust and faith they have established in God. That is one of the worst things that a person could ever do. Our trust in God has to be greater than the life that we build or the boats that we float. The anchor is there to stabilize you. Some people have built lives without faith and without God, and once the storm comes, it pushes them around, because the anchor cannot stabilize them. When we are truly anchored in God, we are unmovable, unshakable and unbreakable, just like David. Once we are anchored with complete faith and total trust in God, our perspective is now God's perspective. Notice

Some people have built lives without faith and without God, and once the storm comes, it pushes them around.

in 1 Samuel 17, David did not take the perspective of others who were afraid of Goliath. Instead, David kept his perspective in line with God's perspective and he knew that he would be victorious in that storm. David told Saul in 1 Samuel 17:36,

> "Your servant has killed both lion and bear; and this uncircumcised Philistine will be like one of them, seeing he has defied the armies of the living God."

When you are fighting in faith, it is important to realize that you have already won the battle. The enemy wants you to doubt that truth, so he will talk tough, bully you, and will incite fear in those around you to cause you to doubt God. God does not work in our doubt. The enemy knows this, and he knows that if you will doubt God before the storm, you are already defeated within the storm. God wants us to be totally convinced in His ability to work on our behalf.

BUILDING YOUR TRUST

One of the best ways to build your faith and trust in God is to trust God with your money. Tithing was instrumental in helping me develop my trust. In every single point of increase in my life over the last 34 years, I have tithed. I have given a dime out of every dollar for over 34 years. I discovered that if you cannot trust God with your money, you will never be able to trust Him with your life. I have discovered that tithing or not tithing is not a money issue, but a trust issue. Many people have iPads, iPods, iPhones and yet they cannot say, "I tithe."

"Honor the Lord with your wealth and with the first fruits

of all your produce..."

Proverbs 3:9

When you give God your first fruits, you are not saying, "God here is my money." What you are actually saying is, "God here is my heart, my trust and my faith."

God does not need our money, but He does want our hearts, and where your treasure is, there your heart will be also (Matthew 6:21). This is extremely important. Begin looking at your finances as fruit that God has given you versus money that you have earned. No matter how little or how much you make every week, God is expecting your first fruits, as a sign of your obedience. By disciplining yourself to do this, you will begin building more faith and more trust in God as you see that He always provides, no matter how little or how much you have.

When you are in a storm, the devil will come to you in many ways. He will fortify an attack by exploiting the issues that you have not conquered in your life and will plant seeds of doubt to cause you to question what you already know about God. If you have not trusted God with your finances, the devil may attack your finances, and when you decide to tithe, he will try to make you believe that you do not have enough to give to God. If prayer has been the area that you have slacked in, once you are in a storm, the enemy will make you feel like it is too late to pray or that praying for your situation is hopeless. In addition, you may feel guilty for going to God simply because you are faced with a problem. I want you to understand that it is important to develop a spirit of faith now through a variety of exercises that will enable you to stand in a storm.

FAITH EPISODES

In addition to tithing, there is a guaranteed way to build your trust in God. Begin with small faith projects or episodes. For instance, if you are going to a mall that is congested, trust God for a parking space right up front. It is important to exercise your faith now with things that are not as big as the "storm" you are going to face in the future.

A great example is to exercise your faith over your headache so that if something major happens like cancer you will have the faith to believe God for your healing. Believe God for relief and healing in the small minor areas and as you begin to see your faith manifest, you will be able to trust God during the big storms. This is why David was able to trust God before the battle with Goliath. Prior to that fight, David trusted God to empower him to kill lions and bears in his father's field when he was a shepherd's boy, so when it was time to fight Goliath, David viewed him as just another lion or bear, not a giant with weapons and a massive army. When we trust God completely, our perspective will be a Godly perspective. In other words, no matter how big your giant or mountain may be, you will know that it does not stand a chance against the almighty power of God. It is imperative you start to develop your God-like perspective over your small faith projects. Realize the arguments, conflicts, gossip that someone may be spreading about you, or money issues that you may encounter do not stand a chance against God. Put those small faith projects in the hands of the Lord and watch great things happen. You will eventually develop a Godly perspective as well as build your faith to a place of complete trust in Him.

Another way to develop your faith and trust in God is by assisting others with their faith projects, through prayers of agreement. Matthew 18:19 says,

"Again I say to you that if two of you agree on earth concerning anything that they ask, it will be done for them by My Father in heaven."

This verse clearly explains why prayers of agreement are important. God responds to them! Pray with others, agreeing on a faith project, and make sure you circle back to receive his/her praise report. I work with a young lady who was facing a storm concerning issues with her business. She had an unproductive business partner, and she was unable to bill clients because their work was not getting done. She exercised two of the faith-building principles in this chapter. She continued to tithe, even as their business bank account was depleting. She also partnered with another sister in faith to fast and pray for her business. Her business partner did not come around immediately, but she did find clarity and courage enough to call her clients to inform them of the current situation. Shortly after that, she began to get leads on additional support that could help her complete some of the projects. After the fast and prayer of agreement, starting that very day, she began to receive a series of calls from new potential clients.

When you develop a spirit of faith before the storm, it will get you through the tough times during the storm. God answers every prayer, even if our prayers are not manifested in the time or manner that we would like. God does not ignore prayers; He answers them and provides His children with a way of escape (when needed), perfect peace, or the ability to weather the storm. Prayers of agreement are important for you. Remember that when two or three are gathered in His name, the Lord is there.

Have you ever been to the gym and tried to lift 200 or 300 pound weights with no prior training? It is virtually impossible. A lot of people hurt themselves when they do this. However, if you start going to the gym a few times a week, and you begin with five pound sets, then gradually increase to 10 pounds, 20 pounds, 30 pounds ……. You will eventually be strong enough to lift weights that surpass your own expectations. After a few months of working out and building your muscles and strength, you will find that your physical strength and endurance have improved. Exercising our faith works the same way as building our muscular system. For most people, it is tough to trust God with everything when they have failed to exercise their faith daily trusting God with the small things. Exercising your faith with daily faith projects will promote your total love and trust in God. The more He meets you right there in your training ground of life, and manifests Himself day after day over the small matters, you will gain more trust in Him. The trust I'm referring to is a genuine type of trust; not the "Oh, it is in God's hands now," type of trust that makes you feel helpless. There is no need to feel helpless, exercising and building your faith muscles will prevent you from reaching a point of desperation, because He has placed all authority in your hands.

Trust your all to God. Do not take anything for granted. Put it all in His hands and graciously thank God when He answers each one of your small prayers or big prayers. Each of us has mountain-moving faith—the raising of the dead kind of faith— the opening the eyes of the blind kind of faith. This was given to us the moment Jesus was crucified on the cross so that we could have victory over every storm. Remember the question is not whether you have faith to face your storm; it is about whether you have been intentional about developing it. It is time to get intentional!

4

WIN WITH THE WORD

Man shall not live by bread [or Popeye's Chicken] alone, but

by every word that proceeds from the mouth of God.

Matthew 4:4

I paraphrased the Word a little, but you definitely get the point. Bread and food are not what sustains us. The Word of God is our substance. The faith principles that we learn in God's Word is the true path to victory. You will win with the Word if you have it stored on the inside of you before the storm. If we look at Jesus, our chief example setter, we notice that in the

Gospel of Matthew, chapter 4, He did not approach the attack or temptation that was on His life with worship, singing, a tithe or offering, but He responded to satan's temptations with Scripture. The Word of God is so powerful,

> *"Sharper than any double-edged sword, it penetrates even to dividing soul and spirit, joints and marrow; it judges the thoughts and attitudes of the heart."*
> *Hebrews 4:12 NIV*

You must involve a daily regimen of the Word in your life, because if you do not have the Word you will not have the faith. Faith begins where the word of God is known. In addition, Faith comes by hearing, and hearing by the word of God. (Romans 10:17) You will be able to release your faith with impact and with power when you know the Word concerning your situation.

I have made the Word of God first place in my life. Each day, we start with the Word. I pull out a scripture, and post it in my bedroom, so that I have a Word to recall throughout the day. In the Old Testament, they kept the Word front and center. In the old days, fathers were responsible for teaching their children God's Word on the way to school. Any true believer, saved, sanctified and a follower of Christ understands that the intake of the Word of God is a regimen we cannot afford to use as a last resort.

Imagine eating a four-course meal. The first course is the appetizer, while the last course is dessert. We must treat our intake for the Word of God just like we treat our intake of food for our natural bodies. The Bible is our appetizer that gets us started, and as we stay in the faith process, with the Word, our victory will be the dessert. We see in the Word of God that our heavenly Father requires us to seek first the kingdom of God. Now the kingdom of God is the order of God. It is a government. It is a system; it is God's way of doing things. The kingdom of God reflects the order of God and the order of God reflects the desire of God. Whenever there is a desire of God, God gives us a design that comes alongside that desire to give it a specific order. God is a God of order. He says let everything be done decently and in order. So we find our orders in the Word of God. It is no different from a man going to a restaurant or a drive through window, and ordering what he desires. Similarly, God has given us orders of what He desires through His Word. The Word and God are one.

A major principle that every believer must understand is that if you are ever going to know God, you must have a relationship with His Word. Unfortunately, you have a lot of people who have greater relationships with things including music or worship, with church, with people and everything else but the Word of God. The fact is that if you are going to overcome, it is the Word of God that will allow you to stand. The Bible says that heaven and earth will pass away, but the Word of God will stand forever.

> **If you are ever going to know God, you must have a relationship with His Word.**

It is absolutely essential that there is a practice of the Word of God in your life. You cannot try to cram a bunch of scriptural references in your mind or try to read a Bible, once a crisis hits. This is the equivalent of trying to fix the levees during the middle of Hurricane Katrina! I have watched it for years, many people have been watching television more than they have been watching the Word, or have been reading novels more than they have been reading the Word of the living God. My greatest appeal is that you make sure that you study to know the Word of God for yourself. It is a practice of mine to be in the Word of God at least two hours every day, whether that is a radio broadcast or a teaching. I am not talking about a radio station where there is gospel music playing, but I am specifically referring to the taught Word of God.

The same amount of time you spend watching reality television, you could be spending in the Word of God and building faith in the Word of God. There are kids who are listening to Lil' Wayne and Drake more than they are listening to Jesus Christ. They can recall all of the lyrics of these songs but cannot recite a Bible verse. We need to spend time with the Word of God more than anything else.

I do not want to appear as if I am putting anyone down; I am just determined to put Jesus up. Lil' Wayne, Drake or Jay-Z have never showed up in the center of any of my storms to help me, but Jesus has showed up to help me every single time. If the storm comes, and I am full of Jay-Z, it is likely that I will not be able to outlast the storm. However, if I am full of the Word, victory is inevitable.

5

RE-ADJUST YOUR THOUGHT LIFE

"For as he thinks in his heart, so is he…"

Proverbs 23:7

There is so much to be said about this component as it relates to the makeup of mankind. You are what you think. The scripture is very clear on that. We are tri-part beings of spirit, soul and body. We are a spirit, we have a soul and we live in a body. Everything about the spirit of man is complete, because it is created in the image of God. It is completely restored and revived and placed back in its original standing with God once you receive Jesus Christ.

"Therefore, if anyone is in Christ, he is a new creation; old things have passed away; behold, all things have become new,"
2 Corinthians 5:17

The body, we know, will always have the effect and impact of sin because of the high treason that Adam committed in the Garden of Eden. Our outward man is perishing day-by-day because of Adam's disobedience.

Now the soul is the central processing unit of man which determines whether that man will live or die, sink or swim, go up or go down. That processing unit is also where he/she will make the decision to win or lose. Although your spirit can be 100% on board with the will of God, there is a change of thought germane to the soul that has to be renewed to God's will. The goal is to get your soul thinking, believing and acting as your spirit would dictate. That is why the Bible says in Romans 12:2,

"Do not be conformed to this world, but be transformed by the renewing of your mind, that you may prove what is that good and acceptable and perfect will of God." The word "renew" is translated as "exchange" or "complete change for the better" (Thayer's Dictionary). There is an exchange of thoughts that must go on in the believer's mind where we have to exchange our carnal thoughts for those of the kingdom of God. This is the only way that we can prove God's good, acceptable and perfect will. As much as we would like Him to, God cannot help us beyond our thoughts. Whenever we want or desire for God to help us in life, He starts by changing our thoughts.

In every municipality or township, they issue an expiration date for each resident's driver's license. The Motor Vehicle Administration (or DMV) will send out a notice to inform us that our license is about to expire and we have to come in and renew it. During the renewal process, there is an exchange of the old license for the new one. Similarly, with our thought life, we have to exchange our old thoughts or BS—meaning belief system (watch it), with a new belief system. The new thoughts that we receive during that exchange, include better, more accurate data, in line with God's will and His Word. During this renewal process, we receive downloads from the Holy Spirit and new data which replaces our old thoughts and data we previously derived from the world. 3 John 2 says, "I wish above all things that thou mayest prosper and be in health, even as thy soul prospereth." Both a man's prosperity and posterity are directly connected to the development of his soul. That word "even" in the scripture denotes a level of equality—meaning the writer wanted us to know that prosperity is evenly distributed throughout our souls, bodies, and spirits.

You cannot go higher than your thoughts.

A man's prosperity or demise in life will be determined by his soul. If your soul stays the same and has not increased through the Word, then your life will never increase and you will always stay the same. You cannot go higher than your thoughts. John Maxwell explains this concept as "The Law of the Lid" in his book The 21 Irrefutable Laws of Leadership, "nothing can supersede (or surpass) the lid or head that it is connected to". In marriage, if a man's thinking is low—if his faith in God is dismal, and his leadership ability is lackluster, the woman, his wife, will literally level off at her husband's lid. It is in the soul or thought life of an individual that will determine how high or low he/she will go in life. One of the major aspects that contributed to the success of my three children was their environment. I talk about the importance of environment a lot, from both the inner and outer perspectives. Externally, you want to hang with people who have your answers, and stay away from those who have your problems; internally, you want to ensure that your mental environment is a reflection of the word of God.

Prior to a storm, you must have your soul fastened. The soul has been referred to as the "anchor." In chapter one, I mentioned that the ship will go back and forth, to and fro with the ways of the wind. But if that anchor is out, it will not be moved. Take a moment to evaluate your soul. Is it anchored, fastened and secured in a position that represents God and growth? Is your soul and thought life secure?

"Blessed is the man

Who walks not in the counsel of the ungodly,

Nor stands in the path of sinners,

Nor sits in the seat of the scornful;

But his delight is in the law of the Lord,

And in His law he meditates day and night.

He shall be like a tree

Planted by the rivers of water,

That brings forth its fruit in its season,

Whose leaf also shall not wither;

And whatever he does shall prosper."

Psalm 1:1-3

MEDITATION

"Blessed is the man who walks not in the counsel of the ungodly—but in his law does he meditate?" Meditation is done in the soul, which is the critical point of our development. We must meditate on the law of the Lord. It is the true way to restore our souls and become anchored in God. You will find that as you read and meditate on the Word, your thoughts will literally become more like God's thoughts—let this mind be in you (Phil. 2:5). Once God is able to download his thoughts into your mind, there will be no storm too tough for you to handle.

ATTITUDE ESTABLISHES ALTITUDE

Attitude is the byproduct of the stability of the soul. The attitude and mindset you have while you are going into anything or establishing anything is literally everything. 2 Corinthians 4:13 reads,

"And since we have the same spirit of faith, according to what is written, "I believed and therefore I spoke, "we also believe and therefore speak."

That spirit of Faith is a lowercase "s," not connoting the Holy Spirit, but instead the attitude of faith that you possess going into a storm or any situation. Just like a thermostat determines the temperature of the room, your position before a storm determines your results and disposition during the storm. Everything may be coming loose at the seams, but a positive, holy attitude will help you stay afloat. I personally believe the statement, "Your attitude will determine your altitude," and it will also determine your outcome. Although nothing may be going right, you can have the right attitude and get the right results. We spoke a little about David's perspective when he was going into the battle with Goliath. Now imagine if David would have had an

> **Your attitude will determine your altitude.**

attitude of disbelief, fear, or instability. He would have lost the battle even before entering. Keep this in mind the next time you are approaching a storm. Your attitude will determine your outcome.

You cannot decide that you want to have a positive attitude

when the heat of hell is at your backside. You have to be positioned to do this prior to your Hurricane Katrina. For instance, when your wife comes home late, or when your supervisor does something to annoy you, keep a positive attitude. It is so easy to offend others when your attitude is not right. But when your disposition is upbeat and positive, you will be able to withstand and endure much more than a person going through the same situation who has a negative attitude.

SO HOW DO YOU DEVELOP THE RIGHT ATTITUDE?

In Philippians 4:8, the Apostle Paul instructs us well:

"Finally, brethren, whatever things are true, whatever things are noble, whatever things are just, whatever things are pure, whatever things are lovely, whatever things are of good report, if there is any virtue and if there is anything praiseworthy—meditate on these things."

Developing a naturally, positive attitude with virtuous thoughts can be attained by meditating on true, noble, just, pure, lovely, good and praiseworthy things. Colossians 3:2 simplifies this by saying, "Set your mind on things above, not on things on the earth." When we are able to see and hear with our spiritual eyes and ears while maintaining a positive disposition, whatever hurricane invades our lives will not be able to uproot us. Your outward attitude will be a direct reflection of your inner thoughts. So check your thoughts, correct your thoughts, and set your mind on things above. You have the power to control your thoughts with the Word.

6

PERFECT THE LOVE WALK

"Though I speak with the tongues of men and of angels, but

have not love, I have become sounding brass or a clanging

cymbal. And though I have the gift of prophecy, and understand

all mysteries and all knowledge, and though I have all faith, so

that I could remove mountains, but have not love, I am nothing.

And though I bestow all my goods to feed the poor, and though

I give my body to be burned, but have not love, it profits me

nothing."

1 Corinthians 13:1-3

When you are establishing a life that is being equipped and

prepared to handle a storm, you must remember to focus on your love walk. The Scripture says that without love, you are nothing. It is essential that we are walking the way that God wants us to walk. His command which supersedes all others except one (love the Lord your God) is "Love your neighbor as yourself," (Mark 12:31). The "love" piece is important in establishing a wholesome life. Preparing your spirit and soul for a storm is about becoming whole, complete and strong on the inside so that the physical characteristics of a storm will not break you. How can we be complete without a heart of love? God is love; and we are made in God's image—therefore we are designed and hard-wired for love. As He is, so are we.

There are four types of love, and many definitions. The first is Eros (the root of erotic) is romantic love. The second is Philia which represents the love found in deep friendship. The third type of love is Storge, the love between family and friends. The fourth and most powerful love is Agape and is considered the highest form of love known as unconditional love. Agape is the type of love that God has for us; it is the strength of who and what God happens to be and everything that the kingdom of

God represents. Imagine ….. what could allow someone to be so forgiving of us when we sin against Him so frequently. It is the only supernatural power that could enable One to forgive and continue loving human-kind, and that is agape love. The idea of extending God-like love and grace to our sisters and brothers is thought to be impossible for some people. Many people have been hurt or wronged so deeply that it affects and infects their ability to love. In order to overcome anything that is contrary to the kingdom of God (storms, illnesses, disease or betrayal), our foundation will have to be established in love.

Dr. Martin Luther King, Jr. once said that love is the only thing that has the ability to transform an enemy into a friend. The transformational power of love in any storm can literally cause something that has the intended purpose of destruction to be turned around for our good. I recently heard a story about a man who was framed for drug possession by a crooked cop. That man ended up serving years in jail and eventually that cop turned himself in and admitted that he had lied. After both the police officer and the accused man had been released from prison, they ended up attending the same church and, can you believe it, they were on the same outreach ministry. The police officer eventually apologized to the man for lying on him and the one who had been accused said the apology was all he needed to be able to forgive him. Now the two are actually friends and have stated that they love each other in Christ. When love is extended, enemies can literally be transformed into friends!

TURN THE OTHER CHEEK

I have watched and experienced many situations, where there was a dispute because of a misunderstanding. The pain of the offense was enough to completely destroy the relationship. Yet when God's love is in action, the ability to love has the power to overcome any disagreement. In addition, it will allow the parties involved to move forward in the relationship as if the offense never occurred. Most of us learned this powerful love principle when we learned the meaning of the phrase, "turn the other cheek." Turning the other cheek is actually a profound spiritual principle that suggests: I want to present to you another side, in order to give you a fresh start. The ability to start over, turning the other cheek, and forgiveness is rooted in love. The Bible says this kind of love demonstrates a level of maturity in the believer's life; perfect love casts out all fear (1 John 4:18). For example, when you are falsely accused, you have to possess a certain degree of love in your heart to move forward. Oftentimes, we get distracted from the things of God and pride causes us to retaliate. Love; however, gives us the ability to see beyond our present state and extend grace to our accusers. This is the same position that Jesus took when He was falsely accused and He remained in love until his Spirit ascended to the heavens. False accusations led Him to being nailed to the cross and while He was in that vulnerable position, He asked His Father to forgive His perpetrators and guaranteed salvation to the sinner. It may have appeared that He had lost, but as Dr. King said, "Truth crushed to the earth will rise again."

When we truly have the "agape" love of God within us, we demonstrate more of Jesus each day. We become more forgiving, understanding and develop the ability to be long-suffering.

DEVELOPING A HEART OF LOVE

How do we develop a heart of love? How do we love others who we feel do not deserve it? We are not called to be doormats but there is a way to love those who have hurt you, even if it is from a distance. Pray for a loving heart and a softer heart that is able to "turn the other cheek." Read the scriptures and meditate on those that provide a model on how to love. 1Corinthians 13:4-7,

"Love suffers long and is kind; love does not envy; love does not parade itself, love is not puffed up; does not behave rudely, does not seek its own, is not provoked, thinks no evil; does not rejoice in iniquity, but rejoices in the truth; bears all things, believes all things, hopes all things, endures all things."

If you could just keep this scripture in your heart during your day-to-day interactions and especially when you are irate and angry, imagine the positive outcome. If you are able to suffer long and be kind, remove all envy and pride, refuse to be rude or evil, then you can inhabit the spirit of Christ. Remain grounded, even when people wrong you and behave in the exact opposite manner that they have treated you. Here is the point to remember about love and forgiveness: if someone has hurt you or

If you can master the love walk before a storm, you will be able to apply that love during hard times.

has hated you, they have been hurt themselves. They have been wounded, and that wound is usually still open. Hurt people truly do hurt other people. Do not continue the cycle by feeding into their hate. Give love instead and break the cycle.

If you can master the love walk before a storm, you will be able to apply that love during hard times. You may have to distance yourself, at first, to get to a place of love and it may be a process, but I want you to truly begin to master this love walk now.

Try This:

Speak 1 Corinthians 13:4-7 aloud, replacing the word "love" throughout this scripture with your first name, and make that your daily affirmation. Here's my version:

"[Michael] suffers long and is kind; [Michael] does not envy; [Michael] does not parade itself, is not puffed up; Michael does not behave rudely, does not seek its own, Michael is not provoked, thinks no evil; Michael does not rejoice in iniquity, but rejoices in the truth; bears all things, believes all things, hopes all things, endures all things." I am love.

7

FAIL NOT TO FORGIVE

"And whenever you stand praying, if you have anything against anyone, forgive him, that your Father in heaven may also forgive you your trespasses. But if you do not forgive, neither will your Father in heaven forgive your trespasses."

Mark 11:25-26

Unforgiveness disguises itself in various forms. For some, it is anger or general bitterness. For others, it leads to depression, and depression leads to anger toward God and others. Many times, people who fail to forgive, take their anger and bitterness out on their family members or those that are closest to them.

Imagine a young woman, for instance, who is raped, and later finds out she is pregnant. That child, who is a product of that rape may live his/her life paying for the mistakes of the rapist. The mother's unwillingness to forgive will have a negative impact on that child forever. One example that we see often, is in families with divorced parents. I do not mean to be stereotypical, but let us just entertain this for a moment. The mother, who is now a single-mom, has children with her ex-husband. Imagine the tension that could arise if those parents have failed to establish a respectful relationship for the sake of the children. How many families do you know with one parent who is still bitter while the other has moved on? Many people who have nasty dispositions because of unforgiveness wonder why they are not happy, and most of the time it is because they have not taken ownership of their own feelings. Unforgiving hearts can ruin our lives and literally snatch our futures away.

Before a storm, it is imperative that you purify your spirit of any and everything that is unlike God. Search deep within your heart and soul—examine your feelings, your unmanaged anger, your snappy or negative attitude and your need for control.

Are these behaviors stemming from deeply rooted seeds of unforgiveness? If so, declare that your journey of total healing and repentance begins now.

Immediately following the prayer of faith in Mark 11:20, is the prayer of forgiveness (verse 25). Forgiveness is the key to everything that faith functions on. If you look at this complete passage, it says that when you pray, you must also forgive. So many people have bottled up anger, offense, and resentment for things that have happened long ago and they wonder why faith

> **Forgiveness is the key to everything that faith functions on.**

principles do not work for them. If you cannot forgive those who have wronged you, how do you expect to be blessed by God? How do you expect to truly activate your faith? Forgiveness is vitally important to the activation of your faith. When you forgive others, your relationship with God is open, free-flowing with no barriers or blockages. Jesus made it crystal clear that we must forgive. Notice that He did not kindly suggest to us to "forgive." He commanded that we walk in forgiveness, because unforgiveness blocks everything known in the kingdom of heaven. Much like a clogged artery that blocks the flow of blood through our veins. In order to have the ultimate level of activation of faith, and that free flowing relationship with God, you must forgive.

> *Jesus said to him, "I do not say to you, up to seven times, but up to seventy times seven. Therefore the kingdom of heaven is like a certain king who wanted to settle accounts with his servants. And when he had begun to settle accounts, one was brought to him who owed him ten thousand talents. But as he was not able to pay, his master commanded that he be sold, with his wife and children and all that he had, and that payment be made."*
>
> *Matthew 18: 22-24*

If there is one area that God is not going to tolerate from a child of His it is unforgiveness. In Matthew 18, Jesus compared the kingdom of God to The Parable of the Unforgiving Servant.

In the text, after the verse cited above, the servant fell on his knees and pleaded with his master to have patience and assured him that he would surely repay his debts. Well the bible says that the master, who was moved with compassion, released him and forgave him of the debt. However, the story does not end there…

"But that servant went out and found one of his fellow servants who owed him a hundred denarii; and he laid hands on him and took him by the throat, saying, 'Pay me what you owe!' So his fellow servant fell down at his feet and begged him, saying, 'Have patience with me, and I will pay you all.' And he would not, but went and threw him into prison till he should pay the debt. So when his fellow servants saw what had been done, they were very grieved, and came and told their master all that had been done."

Matthew 28:31

What do you think happened when the master learned about how evil and wicked this servant, whom he had just forgiven, had been to another man? He delivered him into the hands of the torturers until he could repay the debt. Jesus summed up this teaching by ensuring us that we will receive the same type of treatment, if we fail to forgive.

I pray this resonates with you. I know there may be some deep hurts and heartbreaks that you have faced. Regardless of what has happened and who has wronged you, today is the moment that you are called to forgive. Realize that whatever has happened to you did not destroy you, which means that God is not finished with you yet. Also, understand that we are not called to judge or seek revenge on anyone. That is God's job. By

> **Today is the moment that you are called to forgive.**

harboring anger in your heart toward another person, you are re-traumatizing yourself over and over again, and those who hurt you in the past continue to win. I know a lot of people who have been hurt as children by people that should have protected them. There are women and men who have been manipulated, molested, cheated on and abused. Yes, I realize that your church, or maybe even your pastor, may not have appreciated you—and maybe you feel like you were used for your gifts and then tossed aside. I know. Believe me. I understand how heavy your heart is and how deep this anger may run. But here is what I want you to understand: There is an unspeakable power that lies within the heart of a believer who is able to forgive. You find healing, deliverance, peace and ultimately joy in forgiveness.

JUST LIKE CHRIST

When you are able to love and forgive despite the pain, hurt and betrayal, you are demonstrating the character of Christ. Allow His last moments to sink into your spirit and meditate on His last words. As Jesus hung on the cross, with thorns on his head and blood draining from his body, His last words, through the pain— were, "Father forgive them for they know not what they do,." He interceded on behalf of his enemies. We can learn a lot from our

Lord in that very moment. Not only was He able to forgive the greatest act of hate and injustice in the history of mankind, but He did this despite the pain and torture that his natural body was experiencing. Can you imagine how His flesh must have felt at that moment? He hung there enduring the sins of you and me and everyone before and after us, and He was in excruciating pain. Despite all of that, He endured. His spirit man which he had been feeding for 33 years, rose up and found victory in that moment.

Is your spirit man strong enough to forgive your enemies?

His spirit ignored the flesh, took control and allowed Him to forgive His transgressors. He even asked God to forgive them too. Jesus instructed us to love our enemies, bless those who curse us, do good to those who hate us, and pray for those who spitefully use us and persecute us (Matthew 5:44). Is your spirit man strong enough to forgive your enemies? If so, can you go one step further and also pray for them? This is not merely a suggestion. We are commanded to love our enemies.

THE PROCESS

A month after the acquittal of George Zimmerman (the Florida neighborhood watch coordinator who murdered the unarmed teenager, Trayvon Martin) in July 2013, the BBC published a story that discussed Trayvon's parents healing process following the senseless murder of their son and the injustice that occurred afterwards. A reporter asked Trayvon's mother, Sybrina Fulton, whether or not she and her husband had forgiven George Zimmerman. Mrs. Fulton responded, "As Christians, we have to forgive... but it is a process and we are still going through the healing process. We are still in the process of forgiveness. We know it is coming but we are just not there yet."

In reality, the manifestation of our ability to forgive is present even before the offense. The pain does not determine the forgiveness, but the forgiveness determines the pain, meaning the longer you do not forgive, the more pain you will be in. You may not be over the pain, even after you have forgiven, but still, declare, "I choose to forgive." The pain will respond to your faith.

Forgiveness will not always be easy, but it is necessary. In order to be equipped for a storm, your spirit and soul have to be strong—rooted in faith, love and peace. There is no road to peace that includes unforgiveness. You cannot truly activate faith if you fail to forgive.

"Therefore if you bring your gift to the altar, and there remember that your brother has something against you, leave your gift there before the altar, and go your way. First be reconciled to your brother, and then come and offer your gift."
Matthew 5:23-24

How can we position a platform of overcoming and understanding if we allow unforgiveness to resonate in our lives? Remember that we are discussing the foundation here. This entire book has included lessons that build your foundation of strength and faith prior to your next storm. So again, how can we build a foundation that prepares us to overcome a trial if we are living in direct opposition to the word of God with an unforgiving heart? It is impossible. Jesus made it plain and simple for us through various examples, including Matthew 5:23-24. Here we learn that we are to suspend our prayer time with God in order to reconcile with our brethren. You must get this in your spirit; forgiveness should not be your last resort or your final consideration. Forgiveness should be one of the first steps that you take to prepare your character before the storm.

We rarely have an opportunity to forecast life's major storms. There is no Doppler radar that can predict the severe winds, destructive lightening, or the casualties during a storm. We just simply have to know, because of the Word of God, that we can weather the storm. As we walk by faith, we know that regardless of the nature, speed or force of the winds of life, we will not be shaken or overcome. Instead, we will stand... and stand firm.

"No weapon formed against you shall prosper,
And every tongue which rises against you in judgment
You shall condemn.
This is the heritage of the servants of the Lord,
And their righteousness is from Me,"
Says the Lord."

Isaiah 54:17

STORM PREPARATION CHECKLIST

I HAVE PREPARED WITH PRAYER √
I will start each day with prayer.
I will pray without ceasing.
I will believe in what I have prayed.

I HAVE DECLARED VICTORY √
I will begin declaring positivity over my life.
I will declare after I pray.
I will be intentional about what I speak.

I WIN WITH THE WORD √
I will put the Word of God first.
I will identify a Word concerning my situation.
I will listen to the taught Word of God each day.

I HAVE A SPIRIT OF FAITH √
I will practice faith episodes daily.
I will abandon hope for true faith.
I tithe a tenth to God's kingdom.

I HAVE RENEWED MY MIND √
I will exchange my belief system for God's.
I will spend time meditating on His Word.
I will maintain a positive attitude.

I WALK IN LOVE √
I will represent God the same way He represents me; in love!
I will turn the other cheek.
In all situations, I will demonstrate love.

I HAVE FORGIVEN EVERYONE √
I will no longer harbor resentment, anger or bitterness.
I understand that an unforgiving heart blocks my blessings.
I will demonstrate the spirit of Christ,
by forgiving those who wrong me.

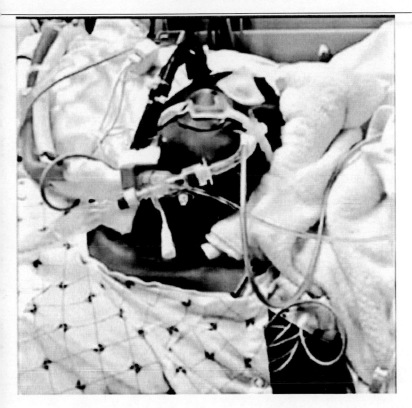

STAY TUNED

If you have enjoyed Before the Storm, get ready for book two in this three-part "Storm" series... Before, During and After the storm. The second installment, During the Storm is Dr. Mike's jaw-dropping personal and family accounts of the storm that threatened his life and global ministries. During the Storm shares important faith principles that will empower you to stand firm, fight in faith, and triumph victoriously during the storm.

Follow @DrMikeFreeman on all social media networks.

ABOUT THE AUTHOR

Bold, compassionate, candid, relatable and kind; these are just some of the words that describe Mike Freeman.

A fourth generation pastor, Dr. Freeman continued his forefathers' legacies when he founded Spirit of Faith Christian Center (SOFCC). He believes his God-ordained assignment is to minister to the whole man - spirit, soul and body – by focusing on faith, family, finances and fellowship. Simply put - Pastor Freeman's heart is to teach people how to achieve God's best for their lives with simplicity and understanding

Founded in 1993, Spirit of Faith Christian Center is one of

the fastest growing ministries in the nation. With three unique locations in Maryland, SOFCC has become home to both pastors and parishioners. Dr. Freeman's profound understanding of the Word of God, coupled with his apparent love for people, have resulted in him being one of the most requested speakers in the body of Christ. He and his wife, Deloris, (affectionately known as DeeDee), have created Marriage Made Easy, a ministry designed to share God's intent for marriage. Pastor Freeman also is the President for, FICWFM (Fellowship of International Word of Faith Ministries), an internationally known minister's organization founded by Apostle Frederick K.C. Price.

The Freemans also share their teachings via Living by Faith, the ministry's television broadcast.

Dr. Freeman enjoys loving relationship with his wife, DeeDee, their three children - Brittney (husband-Kevin), Joshua (wife-Kesha), and Brelyn (husband-Tim), and three adorable "grand-kisses" Dakota, Demi and Joshua, Jr.